PANDA

by Caroline Arnold

Photographs by Richard Hewett

MORROW JUNIOR BOOKS · NEW YORK

The text type is 14 point Berkeley Old Style.

PHOTO CREDITS
Permission to use the following photographs is gratefully acknowledged: Arthur Arnold, page 43; Caroline Arnold, page 6; Jessie Cohen, National Zoological Park, Smithsonian Institution, page 20 (bottom right).

Printed in Singapore at Tien Wah Press.

1   2   3   4   5   6   7   8   9   10

Library of Congress Cataloging-in-Publication Data. Arnold, Caroline. Panda / Caroline Arnold ; photographs by Richard Hewett.   p.   c.m.
Summary: A discussion of pandas with an introduction to those at the Chapultepec Zoo in Mexico City, which features the largest giant panda exhibit outside of China. ISBN 0-688-09496-1 — ISBN 0-688-09497-X (library) 1. Giant panda—Juvenile literature.   [1. Giant panda. 2. Pandas.]
I. Hewett, Richard, ill.   II. Title. QL737.C214A76   1992   599.74′443—dc20   91-33251   CIP   AC

Acknowledgments

We are extremely grateful to Marielena Hoyo Bastien (pictured above), Director of the Chapultepec Zoo in Mexico City, Mexico, for giving us permission to photograph the pandas at the zoo. Without her cheerful cooperation and that of the zoo staff, we could not have done this book. We thank everyone who assisted us there, especially Rafael Tinajero Ayala, zoo veterinarian, for so patiently answering all of our questions, and Florence Diane Murphy Vargas for her kind assistance. We would also like to acknowledge the National Zoo in Washington, D.C., the World Wildlife Fund, the Cincinnati Zoo, and the Mexican Embassy, Washington, D.C., for providing us with information for this project. We thank Carmen Garcia Moreno and all her family for their generosity and helpfulness while we were in Mexico. And, as always, we are grateful to our editor, Andrea Curley, for her enthusiastic support.

We realize that the baby panda, Xin-Xin, may be female, even though we refer to it as "he" in this book. It may be several years before the baby's sex is determined.

3

Seated upright in typical panda style, Tohui quietly munched a stalk of bamboo. From the step of the jungle gym above, her seven-month-old youngster, Xin-Xin (pronounced Sin-Sin), nudged Tohui as if to say "Stop eating and come play with me." It was a warm, sunny day, perfect for climbing and tumbling in the grass.

Like other giant pandas, both Tohui and Xin-Xin have round bodies, bright eyes, and thick, long fur, making them look as much like large stuffed toys as living animals. Their cuddly appearance and gentle personalities make pandas one of the best-loved of all animals. They are also one of the rarest. Without special care to protect the giant pandas and the places where they live, these gentle creatures may soon become extinct.

Grasshopper statue in Chapultepec Park, Mexico City.

Tohui and Xin-Xin live at the Chapultepec Zoo in Mexico City, along with four other giant pandas. Although far from their native home in China, the giant pandas seem happy in Mexico. Comfortable enclosures, plenty of food and water, and good care from the zoo staff provide the pandas with everything they need.

The zoo where the pandas live is located in Chapultepec Park, a large wooded area in the middle of Mexico City. The word *chapultepec* means "grasshopper hill" and, like many words in Mexico, comes from Nahuatl, the ancient language of the Aztecs who once lived there.

Tohui's name means "boy," and is from the Tarahumaras language, which is spoken in parts of northern Mexico today. She was given this name shortly after she was born, and kept it even after the zoo staff discovered that she was female. All the other pandas there have been given Chinese names.

The climate in Mexico City is hotter and drier than it is where wild pandas live in China. At night and in the middle of the day, the pandas at the zoo stay in large rooms where they have platforms for sleeping and space to move around. In the cool hours of the morning and sometimes again in the late afternoon, they go out into grassy outdoor enclosures for exercise and fresh air. Glass panels allow the zoo visitors to view the pandas and let the pandas watch the people, too.

The Chapultepec Zoo has the largest giant panda exhibit outside China. It also has had more success with the natural breeding of pandas in captivity than any other zoo. No one knows exactly why the pandas have bred so well in Mexico, but part of the reason is surely a combination of good care and *buena suerte*, Spanish words meaning "good luck."

The first giant pandas came to Mexico City in 1975 as a gift from the People's Republic of China. They were a young male named Pe-Pe and a female named Ying-Ying. They mated successfully in 1980, but their offspring died after a few days. However, in 1981 these two pandas produced Tohui, who survived. Then, much to everyone's delight, Pe-Pe and Ying-Ying continued to have healthy babies every two years after that. Liangliang, a male, was born in 1983; Xiú-Hua, a female, was born in 1985; and Shuan-Shuan, a female, was born in 1987.

Pandas do not usually live much more than twenty years. Pe-Pe died in 1988 and Ying-Ying in 1989.

Throughout the world, fewer than 100 pandas live in captivity and most of these are in China. Outside of China, only eight countries have pandas in zoos. They are the United States, Great Britain, Spain, France, Germany, North Korea, Japan, and Mexico. Some zoos have only one panda or have animals that are too old to breed. Because there are so few pandas in captivity, it is important to make it possible for those that are of breeding age to mate.

In 1988, special arrangements were made with the London Zoo to send their panda, a male named Chia-Chia, to Mexico City. It was hoped he would mate with Tohui and the other young females that would soon reach breeding age.

On his way to Mexico City, Chia-Chia stopped at the Cincinnati Zoo in Ohio. The extra money that was raised during his visit there was donated to the Chapultepec Zoo and was used to enlarge its panda enclosure.

Chia-Chia arrived in Mexico in November 1988, and in the spring of 1990 he successfully mated with Tohui.

Their baby, Xin-Xin, whose name is a Chinese word meaning "hope," was born at the zoo on July 1, 1990. When Xiú-Hua and Shuan-Shuan reach breeding age, Chia-Chia will have the chance to mate with them, too. With luck, Xin-Xin will be the first of many new baby pandas fathered by Chia-Chia at the Chapultepec Zoo.

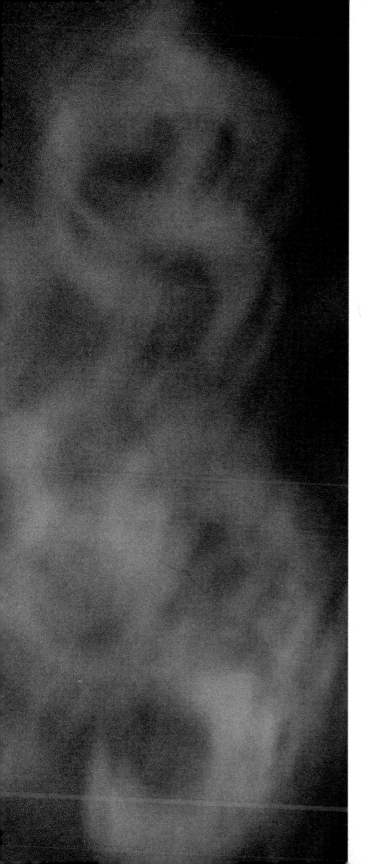

The giant panda is a unique animal with no close living relative. It was once thought that the giant panda was related to a much smaller, raccoonlike animal called the red panda, which also lives in China. Both red pandas and giant pandas eat bamboo and have the same type of teeth. However, in size and appearance the giant panda is more like a true bear such as the American black bear or grizzly. But because giant pandas are not completely like either animal, scientists have decided to classify them in a group of their own.

The scientific name for the giant panda is *Ailuropoda melanoleuca*, which means "black-and-white panda foot." Five sharp claws on each panda foot are useful for digging, climbing trees, or defense. On each of its front paws, a panda also has a sixth "finger" formed from an extension of the wrist bones. A panda can pick up an object such as a bamboo stalk by curling its paw around the object and clamping forward with this extra finger to hold it tight.

In the wild, giant pandas live in the northern and central Sichuan and southern Kansu provinces of China. There the cool, wet climate is ideal for growing the bamboo that pandas need to eat. More than 50 inches (128 centimeters) of rain each year keep the forest moist. Thousands of years ago, bamboo forests grew all over eastern China. Studies of fossil bones show that pandas inhabited a much larger area then, ranging across much of China and as far south as Burma and Vietnam. Over time, the climate in the south and east became drier and the bamboo died out, forcing the pandas to move northward into the forests and mountains of central China, where bamboo was still plentiful. In this century, as the Chinese population has grown and the people have cut down many of these forests to build farms and villages, the pandas have retreated to even more remote regions.

There have been few scientific studies of wild pandas. The first census, or count, of giant pandas was made between 1974 and 1977 and indicated that there were only about 1,100 wild pandas. A more recent survey, completed in 1986, found only 600 to 700 of the animals. About half of them live in protected preserves.

Every year the number of pandas grows smaller owing to destruction of their habitat, accidental deaths in traps set for other animals, and, in some cases, illegal hunting for their skins. Because of their size, adult pandas have few natural enemies except for humans. Baby pandas, however, may be attacked by leopards, foxes, wild dogs called dholes, and large weasels called yellow-throated martens. Despite laws to protect pandas and efforts to preserve their habitat, their plight continues to worsen.

An adult panda is about 6 feet (1.8 meters) long, measured from nose to tail, and usually weighs between 250 and 300 pounds (113.6–136.4 kilograms). In captivity, a well-fed panda can weigh even more. Until they are about four years old, males and females look the same, so even zookeepers cannot tell the sex of a young panda. (No one knows yet whether Xin-Xin is a male or a female.) Pandas are almost fully grown by the age of four, but they usually do not begin to reproduce until they are six or seven.

For the most part, pandas in the wild are solitary animals and rarely interact with one another. Individual pandas usually stay within their own small territories as long as there is plenty of food. Unlike some other animals, they do not defend their few square miles against other pandas. If two pandas meet, they usually just sniff each other and move on. At the zoo, the pandas are usually kept in separate enclosures. Tohui and Xin-Xin will live together until Tohui is ready to mate again.

An adult female panda becomes fertile, or able to become pregnant, for just a few days each year. At this time she is said to be in heat, and only then is she interested in mating. For wild pandas, this mating period occurs sometime between March and May. At the Mexico City zoo the pandas mate in March and April. Beginning in January, adult pandas able to breed are put together for a few hours a day so they can get to know each other.

Female (above) and male (below) giant pandas.

The mountain slopes where most wild pandas live are covered with dense forests. The thick foliage plus misty and rainy weather often make it difficult to see for any distance. One way that pandas find each other for mating is by making moaning, bleating, growling, barking, or squealing sounds. Another way that pandas signal their presence to each other is by smell. Near the base of their short, bushy tails, pandas have two scent glands. They rub their scent on trees or on the ground to mark their territory and to let other animals know that they have been there. At the zoo, the pandas rub their scent on the walls of their enclosures. When a female is getting ready to mate, her scent changes, and the male is attracted by this special odor.

At the beginning of the courtship period, two pandas may feed together in the same area. Although they are aware of each other, they do not get too close. If the male tries to approach the female before she is ready to mate, she may growl to warn him off. If he continues to approach, she may attack him and they may fight. Usually these are not serious

fights, however, and later, when the female is ready, she will accept the male.

After a successful mating, the male and female pandas go their separate ways. The length of the female's pregnancy varies greatly, ranging from 90 to 163 days. When a female panda in the wild is ready to give birth, she chooses a hollow tree or some other secluded place for her nest. At the zoo, a pregnant female is provided with a small cubicle in the corner of her room that she can use as a private nest area.

At birth a baby panda is about 6 inches (15.4 centimeters) long and weighs only 3½ to 5½ ounces (100 to 157.1 grams). The tiny animal is about the size of a stick of butter and has pink skin covered by a coat of fine white hair. The newborn's eyes are tightly shut and it is completely helpless. Although twins and sometimes triplets are born, rarely does more than one baby survive. Even if all her babies are healthy, a mother panda can take only one with her when she leaves the nest to feed. In the wild, baby pandas left alone in the nest usually become victims of hungry predators.

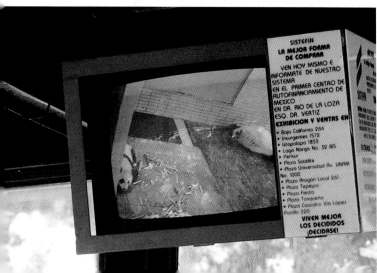

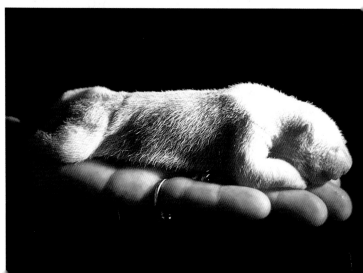

Open doorway leads to Tohui's nest area (top), television monitor (bottom left), newborn panda (bottom right).

For the first four weeks after birth, the mother panda stays in her nest and cradles her tiny baby in her paw to keep it warm and safe. The mother panda rarely puts it down. If the baby becomes uncomfortable, it squeals to get its mother's attention. When it is hungry, the mother panda holds it to her breast so that the baby can suck milk.

As with other mammals, milk is the baby panda's first food, providing the nutrients it needs to grow. A female panda has two teats high on her chest and must hold her newborn in her arm so that it can reach them. She also has two teats lower on her belly, and as the baby panda becomes older and stronger, it learns to crawl to these on its own.

Young pandas grow quickly. By the time Xin-Xin was about six weeks old, his eyes began to open and he weighed about 6 pounds (2.7 kilograms). He was covered with soft, warm, black-and-white fur. At this point Tohui would occasionally leave her baby alone in the nest while she went to another part of the room to eat. Whenever she returned, Xin-Xin would snuggle up to nurse again.

For the first six months after Xin-Xin's birth, he and Tohui spent all their time alone, either in their nest area or in their room. Until Xin-Xin learned to walk, Tohui carried him gently in her mouth whenever they moved from one room to another. The windows of the large room were closed off from public view to give the pandas privacy. During this period, people coming to the zoo to see the other pandas could watch Tohui and Xin-Xin on special television monitors that were connected to a camera in their room. The television monitors also allowed the keepers to watch the pandas and check whether they needed anything. Twice a day keepers brought food and cleaned the room, but otherwise Tohui and Xin-Xin were not disturbed.

By the time Xin-Xin was four months old, he could stand up and walk a few steps on his own. He weighed about 11 pounds (5 kilograms). At six months of age the baby panda's weight had nearly doubled to 21 pounds (9.5 kilograms). The sleeping platform in Tohui and Xin-Xin's room was also a scale. Whenever they climbed onto it, the zoo staff could measure their weight by looking at a gauge outside the room. As Xin-Xin grew, he became increasingly active and playful. One of his favorite activities was to chase his mother's tail. When he got close, he would grab one of her legs like a wrestler. Tohui didn't seem to mind and often rolled around with him on the floor.

Finally, when Xin-Xin was six months old, he and his mother went outside into the exercise yard together for the first time. At first, Xin-Xin always stayed close by Tohui, but gradually the young panda became more independent.

Pandas spend most of their time on the ground, although in the wild they sometimes climb trees to escape from danger or to find a safe place to sleep. At the zoo, Xin-Xin's favorite places to play were the jungle gyms. He was an agile climber and could scramble quickly to the top, where he liked to perform somersaults or hang upside down. Although it looked as if he were doing this just for fun, the exercise helped him to strengthen his muscles and develop his coordination.

During the first few weeks after Tohui had given birth to Xin-Xin, she did not eat at all. A nursing mother panda may lose as much as 50 pounds (22.7 kilograms) during this period when her baby is tiny. However, at this time she is not very active, and she quickly regains her weight once she starts eating again. As Xin-Xin grew older, Tohui ate heartily at each feeding.

From the time that Xin-Xin was about three months old, he liked to nibble a few leaves whenever the keeper brought some bamboo canes for Tohui. At first Xin-Xin would just play with the bamboo. Later, bamboo and other solid food would make up a larger part of his diet.

Tohui will continue to give Xin-Xin milk until he is a year or more old. By the time he is two, Xin-Xin will be able to eat bamboo as his mother does.

In the wild, bamboo is almost the only food that pandas eat. In an area of Chapultepec Park near the zoo, a plot of bamboo has been specially planted for the pandas. Every day someone from the zoo staff goes there and cuts down fresh canes to feed them.

Bamboo is actually a kind of grass, although its tall stalks, or canes, can grow to the size of small trees. There are hundreds of types of bamboo in the world, but pandas will eat only about twenty varieties.

Each kind of bamboo grows for a certain length of time, usually between forty and eighty years. At the end of its growth cycle, all the bamboo plants of the same species all over the world produce flowers, drop seeds, and then die. Sometimes whole forests disappear. It takes several years for the bamboo to grow big again. Usually, when one kind of bamboo dies off, the pandas switch to another variety. However, if the pandas cannot find another species to eat, they starve. This is what happened in 1975, when all the umbrella bamboo in China died and more than 100 pandas starved. In 1983, when the arrow bamboo died, the Chinese launched rescue efforts to save the hungry pandas.

Today, scientists are trying to make sure that there are several different kinds of bamboo growing in the areas where pandas live, so some will always be available when a species dies. They are also trying to establish paths between forests so that pandas can get to other areas when food is scarce in the places where they usually live. The mountain tops where pandas live are like bamboo islands in a sea of developed land. By planting bands of bamboo to connect these isolated forests, scientists are trying to make it easier for the pandas to move between them to find food.

In the wild, pandas spend at least half of each day feeding. Those in the zoo also spend much of their time eating. Pandas have big appetites and can eat up to 40 pounds (18.2 kilograms) of bamboo a day. Although pandas sometimes eat the tender leaf shoots of the bamboo, they prefer the thick stems. Using their strong teeth, they cut these in half to get to the juicy centers.

In addition to bamboo, wild pandas sometimes eat grass, vines, roots, and flowers; honey is a favorite food if they can find it. Pandas in zoos are usually given a more varied diet than that of their wild relatives. At the Chapultepec Zoo, the main food is a mixture of milk, boiled rice, apples, carrots, bread, eggs, meat, and monkey chow. Bamboo is provided as an additional food.

In the wild, the most active feeding periods for pandas are in the early morning and late afternoon. Pandas alternate periods of activity with rest, usually sleeping for about two to four hours at a time.

Unlike true bears, pandas do not hibernate in winter and do not develop a thick layer of fat. Their coarse fur measures about 2 inches (5.1 centimeters) in length. In cold weather, this heavy coat keeps them warm and dry as they search the snowy mountain slopes for food. Bamboo stays green even in cold weather, so pandas can eat it all year round.

In the back of the panda's mouth are large, flat molar teeth. Biting with powerful jaws, the panda uses these teeth to crush tough bamboo stalks. In China, the giant panda is known as da xiong mao (pronounced "dah shwing mahoo"), or "large bear-cat." Like cats, bears, and other carnivores, or meat-eating animals, the giant panda has sharp teeth in the front of its mouth. Although pandas are mainly herbivores, or plant-eating animals, in the wild they occasionally catch and eat small animals as well.

Xin-Xin's first teeth began to come in when he was three months old, and he will have all his teeth by the time he is a year old. Like people, pandas grow both baby and adult teeth. By the time Xin-Xin is fully grown, his baby teeth will be replaced by a set of 12 adult teeth.

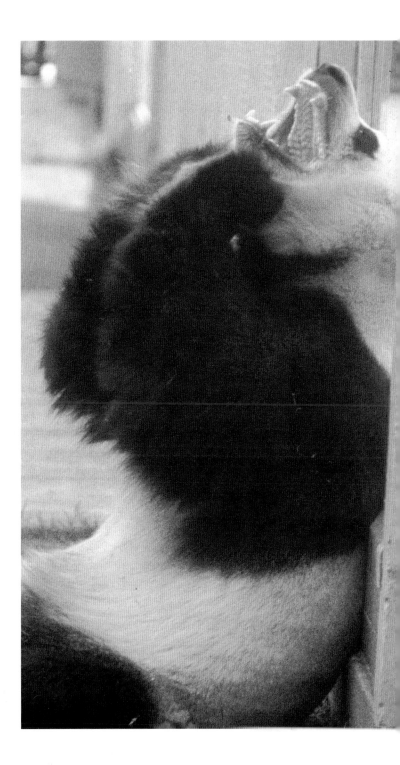

When a panda swallows some food, it first goes to the panda's stomach. From there the food moves through the small and large intestines and the remainder is passed out as body waste. As in the digestive systems of most other mammals, the panda's body absorbs most of the nutrients it needs as food passes through the intestines.

One reason that pandas must eat so much bamboo is that they are able to use only a little of the bamboo's food value. This is because their digestive systems are more like those of meat eaters than those of most plant eaters. Most plant eaters have long intestines through which food passes slowly. This allows most of the nutrients from the slowly digesting plants to be absorbed. A panda, on the other hand, has a short digestive tract. The bamboo passes through it quickly, and only a small portion of the nutrients has time to be digested and used. Plant-eating animals such as cattle and sheep have long digestive tracts and are able to use about 80 percent of the food they eat. Pandas use less than 20 percent of theirs; therefore, they must consume a lot in order to get enough nutrients.

Like all other animals, pandas need to drink water. In the wild, pandas get much of the moisture they need from bamboo, which is 90 percent water. At the zoo, the pandas have water in their rooms. A small pond in the garden area of the panda exhibit provides drinking water when they are outside. Xin-Xin discovered that on hot days the pond makes a good swimming pool as well.

At the end of the pandas' outdoor exercise period, the keepers always let Tohui back into the room first. In that way, Xin-Xin has some time to play outside alone. For part of this time the zoo director comes into the garden, too. Xin-Xin seems to enjoy having a playmate, and by interacting with Xin-Xin, the zoo director is helping him to become accustomed to people. This will make it easier for veterinarians and other people to handle him later when he grows up. As Xin-Xin matures, he will become bigger and stronger. Then it will no longer be safe to play with him.

Xin-Xin is also given a pan of mixed food when he is with the zoo director in the garden. This way the zoo staff can monitor exactly how much he eats and make sure that he gets enough nourishment.

The pandas at the Chapultepec Zoo are loved by people all over Mexico, and thousands come to see them every day. At the end of the exercise period, the zoo director usually brings Xin-Xin close to the window so zoo visitors can get a close-up view of him. Very few zoos have been lucky enough to produce a baby panda, so it is a special opportunity for people to get to know young pandas.

Except for two panda skins and skulls sent to Paris by a French missionary in the 1860s, pandas were little known outside China until this century. The first live panda to leave China was brought out in 1936 by an American explorer named Ruth Harkness. She took her young panda, named Su-Lin, to New York and Chicago. Su-Lin died a year later, but her enormous popularity inspired many expeditions to bring live pandas to other zoos.

One of the crates in which pandas traveled to the National Zoo in Washington, D.C.

Following the Chinese revolution in 1949, pandas were declared to be a national treasure, and they could no longer be exported to other countries. The pandas that live outside China today have been gifts of friendship from the Chinese government.

In 1972, the United States was given two pandas, Ling-Ling, a female, and Hsing-Hsing (pronounced Shing-Shing), a male. They live at the National Zoo in Washington, D.C., which provides them with large, grassy outdoor enclosures filled with climbing equipment, as well as comfortable inside quarters. Like pandas at other zoos, they are a favorite with visitors. Although Ling-Ling and Hsing-Hsing have produced a number of babies, none of them has survived more than a few days.

In the early 1980s the Chinese government stopped giving away pandas. However, during the 1984 Summer Olympics in Los Angeles, California, the Chinese government sent two pandas to the Los Angeles Zoo on a temporary loan. Since then, numerous zoos in the United States have obtained pandas on similar loans.

Recently, such temporary panda visits have created controversy. Some people feel that such exhibits help promote the public concern needed to save the panda from extinction. Also, much of the money earned by zoos during panda exhibits goes to support conservation efforts in China and elsewhere. Others say that moving the pandas around risks their health and safety and that the zoos just want the pandas so they can make more money. One of the problems with allowing a female panda to travel is that it may remove her from a situation where she might breed. A female panda is able to mate for only a few days each year. If the opportunity to mate with an acceptable male is not available when she is in heat, then a whole year will go by before she has a chance to mate again. With so few pandas left, it is important that every female of breeding age be allowed to mate.

In some cases, when a mate is not available for a female panda, zoo veterinarians try to make her pregnant by a method called artificial insemination. This technique involves mechanically taking sperm from a male and putting it into a female. Panda babies have been produced in this way at the Madrid Zoo in Spain and at the Ueno Zoo in Tokyo, Japan. Artificial insemination is not as successful as natural mating for producing offspring. But when natural mating is not possible, it may be better than nothing if there is a chance that a baby panda will be produced.

Pandas visiting the Los Angeles Zoo in 1984.

Usually, a mother panda looks after her baby for about a year and a half. By then the baby weighs about 125 pounds (56.8 kilograms) and can take care of itself. At the Chapultepec Zoo, Xin-Xin will stay with Tohui until the beginning of Tohui's next breeding season. It will be several years after that before Xin-Xin will be able to mate. It is young pandas like Xin-Xin that give hope for increasing the panda population.

The panda is the symbol of the World Wildlife Fund, an international group based in Washington, D.C., that works to protect endangered species all over the world. Scientists from the World Wildlife Fund have been working with Chinese scientists to learn as much as they can about pandas, both in the wild and in captivity. They are also working to preserve the panda's habitat to make sure that the animals will be able to find food and mates.

In the wild, the solitary habits of pandas and the thick bamboo forests in which they live make pandas difficult to study. Pandas that live in zoos, such as Tohui and Xin-Xin, provide a unique opportunity to observe these fascinating and lovable animals close up. With care and hard work, we hope to learn enough about pandas so that future generations will be able to know these gentle creatures, too.

INDEX

Photographs are in **boldface**.